About

Demos is a greenhouse for new ideas which can improve the quality of our lives. As an independent think tank, we aim to create an open resource of knowledge and learning that operates beyond traditional party politics.

We connect researchers, thinkers and practitioners to an international network of people changing politics. Our ideas regularly influence government policy, but we also work with companies, NGOs, colleges and professional bodies.

Demos knowledge is organised around five themes, which combine to create new perspectives. The themes are democracy, learning, enterprise, quality of life and global change.

But we also understand that thinking by itself is not enough. Demos has helped to initiate a number of practical projects which are delivering real social benefit through the redesign of public services.

We bring together people from a wide range of backgrounds to cross-fertilise ideas and experience. By working with Demos, our partners develop a sharper insight into the way ideas shape society. For Demos, the process is as important as the final product.

www.demos.co.uk

First published in 2004
© Demos
Some rights reserved – see copyright licence for details

ISBN 1 84180 122 4
Typeset by Land & Unwin, Bugbrooke
Printed by PrintFlow, London

For further information and
subscription details please contact:

Demos
The Mezzanine
Elizabeth House
39 York Road
London SE1 7NQ

telephone: 020 7401 5330
email: hello@demos.co.uk
web: www.demos.co.uk

Personalisation through participation

A new script for public services

Charles Leadbeater

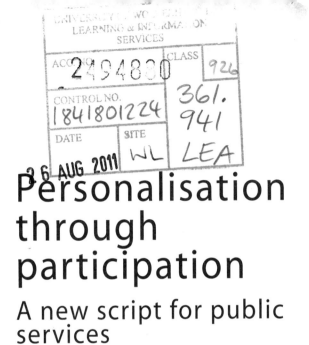

DEMOS

DEM©S

Contents

Acknowledgements

Thanks to Tom Bentley, David Hargreaves, Sophia Parker, Matthew Horne, Paul Miller, and the public services team at Demos, David Miliband, Peter Housden, Jim Maxmin, David Henshaw, staff at Kingston, Blackburn and Liverpool councils, David Halpern, Adam Heathfield, Ed Mayo and Hilary Cottam who all at different times added ideas to this pamphlet through discussions and seminars.

Charles Leadbeater
March 2004

Foreword

This is an important pamphlet about an absolutely vital subject. High quality public services can provide liberation for millions of people. Yet when public services fail to meet popular aspirations, their whole basis comes under threat. This pamphlet engages with the key debate facing politicians, policy-makers, staff and the public – whether we can build a model of public service delivery that overcomes the limitations of both paternalism and consumerism. Since the answer in the pamphlet to this question is 'yes', it is especially important that people engage with its contentions.

As a minister in a public service 'delivery' department, three dilemmas recur as I try to make my contribution to the renewal of public service in Britain. First, how to combine excellence and equity, and more particularly how to use excellence as a battering ram against inequality. The Right say this is not possible. The Left is ambivalent, fearing that a drive to promote excellence as well as tackle low performance might create inequality. Yet it is precisely the excellence that can be developed in the public sector that is both an example of what is possible, and a potential driver of system-wide improvement.

Second, there is the need to ensure universal services are shaped by the personal touch. This is Charles Leadbeater's starting point. I like his answer: engage individuals, alone or in groups, in assessment of need as well as development of service, and you will bring out the best in public service staff, as well as bringing a smile to those who use the service. This requires systems in which innovation and diversity are the order of the day; because people are different, services have to be different.

The third dilemma is about how we get the flexibility that public service staff need if they are to deliver personalised and diverse services, without sacrificing the accountability that is essential if we are to raise quality. The debate within the education system about 'intelligent accountability' points one way forward – more information available to the public, not less, presented in an accessible form. This seems to be what is happening in the health and criminal justice systems too. It should be of benefit not just to the public as 'choosers', but also to public servants as they seek to manage the improvement in performance by learning the lessons of the best.

Each of these three dilemmas echoes through this pamphlet. It is a contribution to the debate not the final word. The recipe of 'basics plus personalisation' may not trip off the tongue, but it speaks to real need and real aspiration. As such, the pamphlet is a significant contribution to the debate about public service reform. It is one which makes me optimistic that as a country we are finding the right ways to use rising investment, and deliver the expansion and

improvement of capacity that the public so
desperately want to see.

David Miliband MP
Minister of State for School Standards

Introduction

On 24 March 2004 the Department of Health made an important announcement heralding impressive reductions in heart disease: between 1997 and 2002 there had been a 23 per cent fall in deaths from diseases of the heart and circulatory system.

Much of this reduction was due to reforms to NHS cardiac services, particularly improved treatment of people who had suffered a heart attack, involving better medicines, technologies and working practices. About 1.8 million people were taking statins, cholesterol-reducing drugs, thus reducing the number of premature deaths per year by 7,000, the department said. But the report also acknowledged that much of the decline in heart disease deaths was due to lifestyle changes that swept the country 20–30 years earlier, when middle class men in particular gave up smoking in their millions.

Contained in this single story are two very different accounts of how the public good is created.

The first account is that the public good – fewer people dying young from heart attacks – comes from the state providing services to society ever more efficiently and effectively. The public good goes up the more effective the state becomes in solving society's problems for it.

The second account is that the public good – fewer people dying young from heart attacks – comes from millions of people making loosely connected decisions in society to change the way they live, which collectively produces a significant improvement in the public good. In this model the state does not act upon society; it does not provide a service. Instead the state creates a platform or an environment in which people take decisions about their lives in a different way. This is bottom-up, mass social innovation, enabled by the state. From this point of view the fact that 1.8

million people are turning to the NHS to get statins is not a sign of success but a sign of failure. It would be far better if these people had lifestyles compatible with low cholesterol, rather than take drugs to deal with the problem after the event.

These two approaches to innovation – more effective top-down and more pervasive and powerful bottom-up – are not necessarily at odds. They could be complementary. Indeed the state's capacity to deliver better and better services, with limited resources, will depend on it encouraging people to become more adept at self-assessing and self-managing their health, education, welfare, safety and taxes.

Yet these two approaches entail quite different accounts of the roles of users, professionals and public service providers. In the first approach the users are patients in need of timely and effective services from the NHS that are personalised to their needs. In the second approach the users are co-producers of the good in question. They are active participants in the process – deciding to manage their lives in a different way – rather than

dependent users. In the first approach the professionals – medical practitioners – must deploy
their knowledge and skills in a timely and
effective way to solve a problem for the user. The
more that is done in a personalised, considerate
and responsive manner the better. In the second
approach the key is to build up the knowledge
and confidence of the users to take action
themselves, to self-manage their health without
turning to the professionals. The professionals
deploy their knowledge to help the users devise
their own solutions – smoking cessation programmes, exercise regimes – which suit their needs.

The differences between these two approaches
to generating the public good go to the heart of
the debate about what 'personalised' public
services should look like.

Personalisation is a very potent but highly
contested and ambiguous idea that could be as
influential as privatisation was in the 1980s and
1990s in reshaping public provision. Privatisation
started as a Conservative policy in 1984 at the
height of neoliberalism but has since been widely

adopted around the world by governments of different political persuasions. Personalisation could have a similar impact and reach because it could provide a new organising logic for public provision, linking initiatives of the first type, more personalised public services, to initiatives of the second type, creating the public good from within society.

Privatisation was a simple idea: putting public assets into private ownership would create more powerful incentives for managers to deliver greater efficiency and innovation. Personalisation is just as simple: by putting users at the heart of services, enabling them to become participants in the design and delivery, services will be more effective by mobilising millions of people as co-producers of the public goods they value.

Personalisation has the potential to reorganise the way we create public goods and deliver public services. But to unlock that potential the idea needs to be taken much further than current government thinking seems to allow. At the moment personalisation seems to mean providing better access and some limited say for users over how existing services are provided in largely traditional ways. This 'shallow' personalisation offers modest modification of mass-produced, standardised services to partially adapt them to user needs. 'Deep' personalisation would give users a far greater role – and also far greater responsibilities – for designing solutions from the ground up. Personalisation could just mean more 24/7 call centres, booked appointments and timely access to standardised services. At the other extreme it could mean promoting greater capacity for self-management and self-organisation. Personalisation could be a sustaining innovation designed to make existing systems more personalised or it could be a disruptive innovation designed to put the users in the driving seat as designers and paymasters of services. It could be a programme to apply a lick of new paint to fading public services or it could be the harbinger of entirely new organisational logic.

Personalised public services could have at least five different meanings.

First, personalisation could mean providing people with a more customer-friendly interface with existing services: 24/7 call centres, booked appointments, guaranteed fast response times, better basic customer service. Public service professionals should be available to users when the users want the service, not the other way around. Given the way that much of the public sector still works, enacting such basic reforms to make it easier for people to get access to the services they want, when they want them, would make a huge difference. This would be a sustaining innovation: it would sustain support for existing services by making them more personalised.

Second, personalisation could also mean giving users more say in navigating their way through services once they have got access to them. Thus in the health service, ministers talk about 'patient pathways' through the system, and in secondary education, children will be given more choice over the pace and style at which they learn. Public service professionals should take more account of users in the way that they deliver the service to them, keeping them informed and giving them ample opportunities to choose between different courses of action.

Third, personalisation could mean giving users more direct say over how money is spent. Users would be given more power to make their own decisions about how to spend money allocated to their education or operation. Public service professionals would not make all the decisions about how resources should be allocated but would have to respond to user demand. A good example is the way some local authorities allow disabled people to commission their own care packages, working with advice from professionals. In this case, the users are far more knowledgeable about what they need and how to get it than many of the professionals. The role of the state is to enable such a managed market in provision to come into being: helping to inform users about available choices and ensuring good quality supply.

Fourth, personalisation could mean users are

not just consumers but co-designers and co-producers of a service: they actively participate in its design and provision. Good examples of this include community safety initiatives, recuperative care programmes for the elderly and many welfare-to-work schemes in which the 'users' actually do a lot of the work themselves because they want to find solutions that do not leave them dependent upon the state. Public service professionals help build up the knowledge and capacity of the users to create their own solutions.

Fifth, personalisation could mean self-organisation: the public good emerging from within society, in part, through the way that public policy shapes millions of individual decisions about how we exercise, eat, smoke, drink, save for our pensions, read to our children, pay our taxes and so on. Many of our biggest social challenges – reducing obesity and smoking, caring for people with chronic health conditions, promoting learning, creating safer communities – will only be met if we promote a mass social innovation within society: self-organising solutions. Public service professionals would help to create platforms and environments, peer-to-peer support networks, which allow people to devise these solutions collaboratively.

As we move from the first to the fifth of these options the implications become more radical and disruptive: dependent users become consumers and commissioners, and eventually co-producers and co-designers. Their participation, commitment, knowledge and responsibility increases. As the role of the user fills out, so the role of the professional must change in tandem. In the first two options professionals are still providing solutions for dependent users, albeit in a more personalised fashion. In the fifth, the professionals are designing environments, networks and platforms through which people can together devise their own solutions.

How far does the government want to go with personalisation? Is it just an attempt to bring better customer service into the public sector in response to complaints about over-centralisation and bureaucracy? Is it an attempt to woo middle class consumers to keep them loyal to public services by giving them more choice? Or is it an idea that could sustain waves of reform, leading from incremental innovations to existing public services but eventually leading to more radical solutions that combine better public services with more capacity for self-organising solutions in society?

The argument of this pamphlet is that once you start personalising public services people will get an appetite for it. They will want more. The genie will be out of the bottle. Rather than contain personalisation the aim should be to take it further and deeper. The aim should not be to sustain existing, often outmoded, forms of provision. The aim should be to disrupt these models and find new, more adaptive solutions. Some will argue that promotion of collaborative and self-organising solutions is a pipe dream, the stuff of open source communities on the internet, Linux and e-Bay, perhaps, or the mutuals and cooperatives of the nineteenth century, but not a modern solution. But go back to the example we started with: heart disease. Further reductions in premature deaths from heart disease will come from more personalised public services. But far more gains will come from persuading people to take more exercise, eat healthier diets, stop smoking and not drink too much alcohol. Future big, cost-effective reductions in heart disease will turn on self-organising solutions: the fifth and most radical form of personalisation set out above. The challenge of personalisation is not just: 'how do we create more personalised versions of existing public services?' The real challenge is: 'how do more personalised public services help people to devise their own, bottom-up solutions, which create the public good?' That is the question this pamphlet seeks to explore.

1. How to help Anne

The fact that Anne Rhodes is still with us is a testimony to public services. Anne was born with cerebral palsy and spent most of her early years shuttling to and from hospitals for operations that saved her life. Thereafter she went to a specialist school for children with learning disabilities. When most people her age were leaving school for jobs or college Anne was directed to an Employment Resource Centre on the edge of her home town, Blackburn. The Centre was meant to provide a secluded, safe environment, in which disabled people could do useful work. On her first day staff asked Anne what she would like to do: make curtains or tapestry. Anne shrugged, not sure that either much interested her, so she plumped for tapestry. She followed that routine every day, for 17 years.

No one ever suggested she do something different. That was all that was on offer.[1]

Anne Rhodes' position sums up the asymmetry at the heart of public services: professionals and providers have the budgets, power and information; users do not. How would the various proposals on offer for improving public services help Anne Rhodes?

One argument is that public services just need more money and staff. Users just want a better version of the existing service, brought 'up to date'. That would mean giving Anne Rhodes better needles, thread and thimbles, a better way to do tapestry: something she never wanted to do and which has yielded few benefits for her or wider society.

A second argument is that Anne should be set free as a consumer, with the funds to buy services to suit her needs. Producers would have to respond to her demands. Yet Anne Rhodes finds it difficult to walk around, let alone shop around. She is bright but short on confidence and finds it hard to communicate. Liberating her as a consumer would take far more than giving her a wad of money and the freedom to spend it.

A third argument is that Anne should be seen as a citizen. The key feature of public services is that they are collectively funded, with priorities set by democratic decision-making. Anne's service might be changed if she had a voice in its governance through a seat on the centre's management committee. But Anne is not used to being on committees and she does not want a voice in the running of the whole centre; she wants to be able to influence her service, directly and immediately. The offer of citizenship is too vague and distant to offer her any real prospect of changing the kind of service she receives.

None of these proposals for reorganising public services – reinvestment in existing services, consumer choice, citizenship and voice – would make much of a difference to Anne. What did Blackburn Council do when they took over the centre from Lancashire County Council in 1998?

Blackburn offered Anne an opportunity to personalise the service she received by giving her the opportunity to participate in its design and delivery. We need to understand what is distinctive about how the council did this because this simple model could be a part of every aspect of public service provision. Personalisation through participation, the approach staff in Blackburn came up with instinctively, offers a more promising avenue for public service reform than any other currently available. Here is how it worked in Anne's case.

First, staff running the centre started an intensive, intimate and lengthy conversation with their clients to find out what they wanted to do. It was the first time in 17 years Anne had been asked what she wanted. Staff said their goal was for people using the centre to have the opportunity to become more independent, to gain the confidence to stand on their own two feet. They drew up a range of training options Anne might consider. That limited opportunity to exercise choice and ambition then unlocked Anne's voice. She told the staff she had always wanted to get a job but had never realised she might be able to do so.

Every Wednesday for six months, Anne went to a pre-vocational training course run by Manchester Open College, designed to help people get ready for taking a job. When she finished the course, staff from Anne's centre organised for her to work an afternoon a week in a nearby council nursery. After six months Anne and the staff at the nursery want her to work more often. Anne wants to go on more courses.

'I feel normal for the first time in my life,' Anne explained. 'I am part of society not on the edge.'

Anne's life was transformed only because staff took the time to help her articulate the intricacy of her needs, gave her enough choice to voice her aspirations, and organised relationships with training providers and other partners to create a solution for Anne that the centre could not have delivered. Crucially, Anne was an active, informed and increasingly articulate participant in this process: the solution was personalised through participation. As a result Anne felt more committed to the service than she had been when it was delivered to her as a passive, dependent consumer.

Public service reform should be user-centred. It should be organised to deliver better solutions for the people who use the services. But it must also, in the process, deliver better outcomes for society as a whole: effective collective provision to meet the need for education, health, transport, community safety, care for vulnerable people. The challenge is to build these two sources of value – for the individual users and the wider society – together. The combination creates public value. Treating users as atomised consumers ignores the wider social influences on the choices they make and the wider consequences of their choices, for example, over which school to choose for their children. Treating people as citizens, who can reshape services through formal political debate, is worthy but abstract. Only policy wonks think people will be excited by attending more meetings. Users want direct attention to their needs.

That is why we need a new framework to show how personal needs can be taken into account within universal, equitable public services, how effective collective solutions can be built up from millions of personal decisions. The starting point is to rethink what services are and how they generate value.

In the process we also need to develop a new story about how change occurs in institutions and public service organisations – how they can reshape themselves through repeated interaction with the people they serve and continuous effort to find better ways of serving them. This story needs to make sense for service users and practitioners, but it also needs to be incorporated into the way politicians and civil servants understand and undertake large-scale reform. It needs to be a story of what role the state plays in creating public goods in a society in which people want more choice, more voice and more scope for self-organisation.

2. Services as scripts

Our models of production and consumption are still dominated by industrially produced goods – cars, stereos, washing machines – the physical and technical characteristics of which can be easily defined and compared. Shopping around for a washing machine in the basement of John Lewis involves comparing fairly standardised goods. Our images of what it means to be a consumer are still dominated by this shopping mall idea of choosing between different physical goods.

This model is inappropriate for many services. True, more services are now standardised: witness telephone banking or fast food restaurants. But services that generate personal satisfaction or solve personal problems – whether public or private – are far more difficult to define in quantitative terms. It is difficult to shop around for something that cannot be defined easily and to be effective has to be designed with you in mind.

Services should be seen as scripts. All services are delivered according to a script, which directs the parts played by the actors involved. The script for eating a meal in a restaurant is: reserve table, arrive at restaurant and be shown to table, examine menu, place order with waiter, food delivered to table, eat, ask for bill, pay, leave. Service innovation comes from rewriting scripts like this so the action unfolds in a different way. A fast food restaurant runs on a different script: read menu, place order for food, pay, take food to table yourself, eat, clear away your debris, leave. In a full-service restaurant you eat and then pay, and do very little else. In a fast food restaurant you pay and then eat, and contribute some of your labour by taking the food to the table and clearing away your mess.[2]

Most service innovation comes from producers and users simultaneously adopting a new script, playing out new and complementary roles in the story. It is very difficult for service producers to innovate unless the users also adopt the new roles in the script. Increasingly innovation comes from consumers deciding to write new roles in their script for themselves and insisting that the producers respond. That is the story of the rise of SMS messaging. Mobile phone companies had a script for how SMS messaging would be used: in emergencies. But teenage users of mobile phones invented a new script and with it a new service and new uses for mobile phones. The producers have had to respond to the script that was collectively written by the users. Service innovation is invariably a joint production combining producers and consumers.

Often radical innovation involves bringing together ideas from quite different scripts: the telephone service script (used in banking) and health care knowledge, when brought together, created a new script for accessing health advice in the form of NHS Direct. The old script was: phone GP, make appointment, visit surgery. Now there is a new script, which starts with a phone call to NHS Direct asking for help.

Many of the scripts followed by public services – such as schooling – have not changed for decades: enter classroom, sit at desk, listen to teacher, read from blackboard, write in exercise book, hand in work, run to playground. The scripts for user engagement with the police, health services and libraries are largely written by professionals, producers and regulators, not by users. The users are expected to fit into the roles given to them by the script handed down from on high.

How should we rewrite the scripts for public services?

3. Better basics

One answer is that service scripts need rewriting to make them simpler, more efficient and responsive. Most people want reliable, timely basic services: trains that run on time, bins collected, housing repairs done swiftly, planning decisions taken quickly. It is not rocket science. Nor is it simply about more investment. The scripts by which services are delivered need rewriting. One problem with public services is that the number of people and departments involved makes services bureaucratic, unresponsive and slow moving.

A good example of how service scripts can be made simpler and more responsive is Liverpool Direct, the joint venture between the city council and BT to create a new way for users to access services. The venture, created in 2000, is due to run over 11 years. BT put in an initial investment of more than £60 million to create the technology platform for a call centre, web access and to integrate IT systems. The Council pays the joint venture about £30 million a year to provide it with services. As a result users can call the Liverpool Direct call centre 24 hours a day, seven days a week, all year. The centre is getting more than 50,000 calls a month. It has, quite literally, given users a voice in their services.

Take just two examples. The children's social services team used to miss more than 50 per cent of the calls made to it, mainly because social workers were out making visits and the answer machine in the office got overloaded. If you called for help, it was a lottery as to whether your call would be logged let alone dealt with. Now the council's dedicated Careline service means that less than five per cent of calls are missed. Social services workers sit alongside customer care operatives in the call centre so that decisions can be made while the caller is on the line. It used to take two days to allocate a social worker to a case.

Now it takes an hour. Or take the more mundane example of bins. The council's refuse collection service used to miss thousands of bins, in a collection round of more than 200,000 a week. Now the proportion of missed bins is less than 0.1 per cent. Part of the explanation is that users can now get through to the council to complain about an uncollected bin. In the past most of their calls were not taken.

Liverpool Direct is a tangible example of how users have been given more say in their services. But that is just the starting point. To deliver on Liverpool Direct's promises, services have been re-engineered to make them simpler, swifter and more responsive. Eleven different people had to be involved in making a decision before a pest control officer would visit a property to sort out a rat infestation. Now the pest control officer can be allocated, with an appointment made over the phone, from the call centre.

The scope for basic improvements to public services – giving users a more direct and effective voice and streamlining services to make them more responsive – is vast. Yet even these basic improvements involve more than just doing the same things a bit faster, with better equipment. Liverpool Direct shows that better basics come from redesigning services from scratch, rethinking the roles of professionals and other staff, even creating a new organisation to deliver services.

Improving the basics, while necessary and possible, may reduce dissatisfaction with poor services without creating satisfaction. Research by Mori on attitudes towards services shows that users are dissatisfied with services if they are inaccessible, unreliable, unfriendly or lacking in competence.[3] To eliminate dissatisfaction you have to do the basics well by providing reliable, timely, competent services. However, once those dissatisfaction factors are eliminated, further focus on them may not create growing satisfaction. Take bins as an example. People want their bins collected on the same day every week, preferably around the same time. When that does not happen they grumble. But providing them with a 15-minute guaranteed time slot when their bins will be collected may not further increase satisfaction.

Some public services are starting from a low base: the task is to eliminate blatant sources of dissatisfaction by doing the basics better. If the Liverpool approach is right this involves giving users a far more direct voice in services and rewriting the delivery script around their needs. Ventures such as Liverpool Direct provide a basic level of personalisation: appointments, guaranteed response times. But to generate more value and more satisfaction, public services will need other approaches.

That means government has to play a more creative role. But if central government intrudes too far into people's lives or imposes solutions it will run into opposition. In a liberal, open society, the government's chief role is to encourage the emergence of collective solutions from within a society that wants greater scope for self-organisation and bottom-up initiative. It has to find a new marriage between the top-down and bottom-up organisation of public goods such as education and health. Where are we likely to find such a marriage? Some believe the answer will be found by encouraging public service users to become consumers.

4. Consumerised services

This morning I bought a watch. I did not have to tell anyone in advance. I did not sign any forms, nor did I have to get a watch-buying licence. Around the world about 40 million other people probably bought watches today, each of which required components to be made, faces printed, packaging shipped. The producer and retailer of the watch did not know I was going to buy it. They did not have to know anything about me. There was no grand plan to organise the production. I did not have to put my name down on a watch-waiting list. The market that brought me together with my watch also coordinated millions of other decisions that organised the production of millions of watches. The fact that we can coordinate this complex web of individual decisions without anyone having a plan or being in charge is why it is difficult to be against market-based consumerism for products such as watches.

Consumer choice is a good thing in markets that trade goods and services where property rights are relatively clear, products are relatively easy to compare, consumers can gather information easily and there are many buyers and sellers of services. For products such as cars, stereos, computers, bank accounts, and airline tickets, markets that allow consumers choice are the best way we have found to organise economic life. Consumer choice sends signals about what people want that producers should organise themselves around. In theory at least, this means that resources can be reallocated to reflect consumer demand rather than reflecting what producers decide should be made. Consumers who are well informed, able to form clear preferences and easily exercise those choices in the market are the arbiters of value.

Providing users with greater choice would shake up the public sector. As Andrew Turnbull, the Cabinet Secretary, said in a recent speech:

> *People have written about disruptive technologies. I would describe choice as disruptive governance. It really forces you to change your view of the world. It is at this point that power really shifts. It is like that inversion of magnetic north to magnetic south that scientists talk of, where accountability for the first time really starts to flow downwards.*[4]

Why shouldn't elderly patients have a choice about where and when they get a hip operation done, or parents more choice, within the public sector, about the curriculum and ethos of the school their children go to? Or take social care packages for elderly people provided by social services: why shouldn't the user make the choice about what mix of home-based services they want, given the budget available? Why is the public sector so frightened of the choices that its users might make?

In some services it makes sense to put consumers directly in charge of commissioning the service they want, especially where consumers have far greater knowledge than professionals about what they need and what might be available. A prime example is the expansion in direct payments to disabled people to allow them to commission their own home care packages suited to their needs. In Kingston, a council that pioneered this approach, Roy Taylor, the Director of Community Services, explained how it works:

> *Disabled people tend to be really well informed about their conditions, what they need and where to get it. We've established a body with the voluntary sector to help advise them and to help organise the market. But by and large disabled people are in a better position to know what they need than we are.*

People in Kingston with disabilities are entitled to independent living direct payments to then employ their own personal assistants. They do so in conjunction with the Kingston Centre for Independent Living. Independent living centres across the country have formed a self-help network which has borrowed ideas from similar networks in Canada which have as their goal: 'individual and community-based change which promotes self-determination and full participation in society for people with disabilities.' The Canadian centres are largely staffed and governed by people with disabilities.

Making a reality of choice in other services would require far-reaching changes, not least to financial flows. If a patient were able to choose from among several hospitals for an operation, that choice would be frustrated if the money did not flow to the hospital he or she chose. To make an informed choice the patient would need much better information, including the performance of individual surgeons and wards. Capacity would need to shift in response to demand: organisations that became more successful and popular would need to be able to increase their available capacity to meet demand, otherwise queues would just lengthen.

Consumer choice would be a challenge to the power of professionals and providers to allocate resources to services. But the extent to which public services can be driven by consumer choice also has limits.

○ Consumerism assumes competition that allows consumers to choose between competing options. But in some public services – policing for example – it does not make sense to have competing providers, using competing infrastructures. Competition would lead to waste and inefficiency.

○ Consumerism works where goods and services can be packaged and priced. Yet the goods and services the public sector provides are not always neatly packaged in the way that stereos, cars and computers can be. Many public

services are fuzzy, difficult to define
and pin down, for example the value
of community safety. The qualities of
these public goods cannot be assessed
and encapsulated in the way that the
features of a computer can be
described in technical language.

○   Consumerism is based, at least in
theory, on individual preferences. But
in public services it is often difficult to
separate one individual's preferences
from another's. Parents choose schools
in part based on what other parents do.
Simplistic models of consumer choice
fail to take into account these social
and environmental factors.

○   Consumerism works when consumers
have good information about service
performance. But in the public sector
most information, and the ability to
interpret it, is in the hands of
professionals and staff. Users rarely
have all the information they need –

about possible costs and benefits of different forms of health treatment for example – to make a fully informed decision.

O   As choice expands, the costs of searching across competing offers rises. As diversity expands it becomes more difficult to compare different services. Choice imposes costs on consumers as well as benefits.

O   Market consumerism applied to public services could threaten the principles of equity on which public services are based. Public service goods such as health and education are essential to the quality of people's lives and their ability to play a full role in society. These foundational goods should not be distributed by ability to pay but according to need.

Further extension of choice of the kind some disabled people now enjoy should be a vital component in public service reform. But given the difficulties involved, choice cannot provide a sole organising principle for a reform strategy. Users of public services want to be treated well, as customers, but that does not necessarily mean they want to become consumers, shopping around for the best deal or even threatening to do so. We need to find a way to make public services responsive without turning the public sector into a shopping mall. We need a way for users to be treated with respect and consideration when they cannot exercise the sanction of taking their business to another supplier.

5. Citizen-led services

Many on the centre left are attracted to the idea that service providers should respond to the views of citizens. There are good reasons why public services should be organised around the priorities of the citizen:

O   Citizens fund public services through taxation and their participation in the democratic process can have an influence over how that money is spent.

O   Citizenship speaks to the ideals of equity and collective provision embedded in public services. People generally want good public services for everyone, not just for themselves.

O   Using a public service is not just a consumer experience. Each

> engagement with a public service
> should deepen a sense of civic
> attachment and underpin a sense of
> citizenship: why it matters to be part
> of a democratic society.

The centre left likes the notion of citizenship because it speaks to the 'higher' side of people's lives – their participation in democracy and the pursuit of equity. Research has shown that about 77 per cent of people see the NHS as a universal service, that should not be just for the poor.[5] The Institute for Fiscal Studies found that support for universal public services did not fall even among those who had opted to pay for private provision: by and large they still agreed with the *ideal* of universal public services.[6] People seem to recognise that the quality of public services they get cannot be detached from the experience other people get: they are in it together. That is why democratic decision-making over collective provision makes such sense.

Yet citizenship cannot, on its own, provide a

good guide to how public services should be organised day by day. Users of public services do not want a 'voice' in their management or periodic opportunities to have a say on how public funds should be spent. They want a good service, which is efficient, responsive to their needs and treats them with respect.

No amount of talk about citizenship will empower consumers in their day-to-day engagement with public services. Nor does it provide public sector managers with a clear enough sense of purpose in deciding how to run services. Leading Labour-controlled councils, such as Gateshead, which displays a powerful sense of civic purpose embodied in the Baltic Flour Mills Centre for Contemporary Art for example, also have highly developed programmes to focus on customer satisfaction. Managers in hospitals, libraries, schools and police stations need a tangible set of goals linked to what users need, here and now. Users want better services, not more meetings at which they can discuss plans for better services. As Tom Bentley puts it:

> *We would be optimistic in the extreme to think that simply applying time-honoured methods of formal representation and voting to a wider spread of institutions is likely to engage a critical mass of the population. The logic is that police forces, schools, councils and so on could become more visibly responsive, and that more direct participation in deliberating over the complexities of public decisions would spread a new found appreciation for public life among a currently disengaged public. As a sole basis for political renewal, this is a slender hope.[7]*

Voice for users – the more direct, informal, immediate the better – is a vital component in public service reform. But citizenship – formal democratic representation – cannot be the sole organising principle for public service reform. Instead, we need an approach that gives people a direct voice through the *way* in which everyday services are actually developed and delivered.

6. Personalisation through participation

Personalisation through participation makes the connection between the individual and the collective by allowing users a more direct, informed and creative say in rewriting the script by which the service they use is designed, planned, delivered and evaluated. In the case of Anne Rhodes and other emerging examples of participative services, this invariably involves these steps:

O **Intimate consultation:** professionals working with clients to help unlock their needs, preferences and aspirations, through an extended dialogue.

O **Expanded choice:** giving users greater choice over the mix of ways in which their needs might be met; to assemble solutions around the needs of the user rather than limiting provision to whichever institution in question – the school, hospital, social services department – the user happens to be closest to.

○ **Enhanced voice:** expanded choice should help to further unlock the user's voice. Making comparisons between alternatives helps people to articulate their preferences. This is very difficult to do from a blank sheet of paper. Choice helps to unlock voice.

○ **Partnership provision:** it is only possible to assemble solutions personalised to individual need if services work in partnership. An institution – for example a secondary school – should be a gateway to a range of learning offers provided not just by the school but by other local schools, companies, colleges and distance learning programmes.

Institutions should be gateways to networks of public provision.

○ **Advocacy:** professionals should act as advocates for users, helping them to navigate their way through the system. That means clients having a continuing relationship with professionals who take an interest in their case, rather than users engaging in a series of disconnected trans-actions with disconnected services.

○ **Co-production:** users who are more involved in shaping the service they receive should be expected to become more active and responsible in helping to deliver the service: involved patients are more likely to attend clinics, students to do homework. Personalisation should create more involved, responsible users.

○ **Funding:** should follow the choices that users make and in some cases – direct payments to disabled people to

> assemble their own care packages –
> funding should be put in the hands of
> users themselves, to buy services with
> the advice of professionals.

Users should not be utterly dependent upon the judgement of professionals; they should be able to question, challenge and deliberate with them. Nor are users merely consumers, choosing between different packages offered to them; they should be more intimately involved in shaping and even co-producing the service they want. Through participation users have greater voice in shaping the service, but this is exercised where it counts, where services are designed and delivered.

Service users can only change their role in the service script, however, if professionals alter theirs. Professionals have to become advisers, advocates, solutions assemblers, brokers. The role of professionals in participative services is often not to provide solutions directly, but to help clients find the best way to solve their problems themselves.

Can personalisation provide an organising principle for public service reform?

Table 1 compares how personalisation would provide a new organising ideal for public services, in contrast to traditional public sector management and new public management, which became fashionable in the 1980s, with its emphasis on contracted services.

There are important public services where personalisation will not make sense. Someone entering an accident and emergency department does not want a dialogue, they want quick, competent treatment. Defence, traditionally conceived, is not something that can be personalised, although the public has a vital role to play in the fight against terrorism, for example.

Personalisation will make sense most in services which are:

O   Face to face: education, non-
      emergency health care, social services,
      housing

Table 1 A new organising ideal for public traditional public sector, new public

	Traditional public sector
Public interest	Defined by politicians and experts
Performance objective	Manage inputs Good administration
Accountability	Upwards through departments to politicians
Delivery model	Public institutions Professional self-regulation Hierarchical departments
Ethos	Patrician public services Technocratic

services: comparison between management and personalisation

New public management	Personalisation
Aggregate customer preferences/customer surveys	Dialogue between providers, funders and users at all levels
Inputs and outputs managed for efficiency	Multiple agreed with stakeholders, users including user experience and social value
To politicians and users through market comparisons and contracts	To users directly as well as taxpayers, stakeholders and politicians
Contracted services	Mixed market of providers. Solutions assembled from a variety of sources around user needs
Market-based	Democratic, personalised, user-centric

continues overleaf

Table 1 continued

	Traditional public sector
Users	Deferential
Manager's goals	Satisfy political masters, professional self-regulation
Private role	Minor, kept separate
Professional role	Decide and allocate resources
Classic organisational form	Reithian BBC The central Civil Service

Source: Adapted from *Creating Public Value*, Strategy Unit.

New public management	Personalisation
Consumers, some self-service	Co-producers, creating solutions with professionals
Meet contracted performance targets	User satisfaction, wider social benefits
Major role in service delivery	Public good comes from combination of public and individual initiatives
Commission and monitor	Advise, broker, advocate, solutions assembler
Wandsworth Council 1980s Next Steps Agencies	SureStart, welfare-to-work, direct payments to disabled

○ Services based on long-term
relationships between users and
producers, rather than a set of
transactions, for example the
management of a chronic disease

○ Services that depend on a direct
engagement between professionals
and users where the user can play a
significant role in shaping the service.

A good example is health care, where surveys show 80 per cent of patients want more involvement in decisions about their treatment, particularly in the long-term treatment of conditions such as diabetes. In one study of two groups of 100 diabetics, those with traditional, professionally administered care were far more likely to have crises and require hospital treatment than those who were trained to self-manage their treatment and self-monitor their condition. Almost 70 per cent of those dependent upon professional help had crises, compared with only ten per cent of the self-managers. The

Department of Health estimates the average diabetes sufferer sees a doctor for perhaps three hours a year and provides thousands of hours of self-care. Spreading the capacity for self-care will do more for diabetics than increasing the number of doctors. As the population ages and chronic and long-term conditions become more prevalent it will become more important to create a widely and equitably distributed capacity for self-management, at home.

'Personalisation through participation' in public services means users having a far greater say in writing the scripts for how their services are delivered, so that they have some say about the order in which things happen, how the story might branch, take different routes and end. As a result the users are more involved but also more committed and more likely to take their share of responsibility for ensuring success. At the same time, professionals are able to apply expert knowledge or evidence in far more flexible, or differentiated ways – by combining different elements of a package according to the needs and preferences of the user, which are much clearer and more explicit as a result of their involvement in the process.

One of the largest applications should be in education. Personalised learning would provide children with a greater repertoire of possible scripts for how their education could unfold. At the core there would still be a common script – the basic curriculum – but that script could branch out in many different ways, to have many different styles and endings.

The foundation would be to encourage children, from an early age and across all backgrounds, to become more involved in making decisions about what they would like to learn and how. The more aware people are of what makes them want to learn, the more effective their learning is likely to be.

Young people are far more avid and aware consumers than they used to be. This culture is bound to have an effect on how they view education. Many secondary school age children now have mobile phones for which they can get

24/7 telephone support, different price plans, equipment and service packages. They are used to a world in which they can search for, download and share digital music on the internet. Children have quite different kinds of aptitude and intelligence, which need to be developed in quite different ways. The school system already recognises that some children have 'special' needs and so need personalised kinds of learning environments and teaching styles. But up to now the system as a whole has been unable to deliver this flexibility consistently for all those who need it, or to integrate children with special needs into the 'mainstream'. Personalised learning would extend this principle, already implicit in the system, to all children. Equity cannot be handed down from on high in a society with a democratic culture in which people want a say in shaping their lives. Comprehensives promoted equity through common standards. 'Personalised learning' allows individual interpretations of the goals and value of education. Children should be able to tell their own story of what they have learned, how and why, as well as being able to reel off their qualifications, the formal hurdles they have overcome. Their personal involvement in making choices about what they learn, how and what targets they set for themselves, would turn them into more active learners.

Personalised learning does not apply market thinking to education. It is not designed to turn children and parents into consumers of education. The aim is to promote personal development through self-realisation, self-enhancement and self-development. The child/learner should be seen as active, responsible and self-motivated, a co-author of the script which determines how education is delivered.

The traditional script, largely written by producers and regulators, is that education proceeds through a series of stages, which set the rhythm for how people learn, at what pace and to what end. In many ways the standards agenda of the 1990s has made these scripts more uniform – the literacy and numeracy hours in primary schools – for example.

Personalised learning would start from the premise that learners should be actively, continually engaged in setting their own targets, devising their own learning plans and goals, choosing from among a range of different ways to learn. Experiments with pupil self-assessment and target setting – for instance at Nine Stiles, a comprehensive school in Birmingham – show that pupils do not set themselves targets that are easy to reach. They tend to set realistic but stretching targets.

New approaches to assessment, for example 'assessment for learning', help learners work out how effective their learning was, what worked well or badly for them. That allows students to adjust and adapt their learning strategies. Traditional assessment tests the extent of someone's knowledge at the end of a period of learning and provides the learner with little information about which learning strategies were more effective. Personalised learning would only work if students were engaged in continual, self-critical assessment of their talents, performance, learning strategies and goals. Personalised learning would allow and encourage learning to take place in holidays and outside normal school hours. It would make opportunities to learn available whenever the learner wanted to take them up. Children would be able to take time out for other activities that might add to their learning: voluntary work, drama and sports. This flexibility might be based on the principle of 'earned autonomy'; children who clearly do well and are self-motivated become more self-regulating. Students should have a choice – under earned autonomy – about where learning takes place: at home; at an individual school; moving among a network of schools; virtually through ICT in school, at home or in a third space such as a library; *in situ* at a workplace or voluntary group.

This implies far-reaching changes in the roles of professionals and schools. Schools would become solutions assemblers, helping children get access to the mix and range of learning resources they need, both virtual and face to face. Schools would have to form networks and federations which shared resources and centres of excellence. An individual school in the network would become a gateway to these shared resources. What does this mean for funding of education? Should each school get a set sum per child? Should the money follow the student? Should all students have an amount they can spend on learning materials from outside the school? All these options have complications. Yet if money does not flow with student choices then the system will not be truly responding to learner demand.

A mass, personalised learning service would be a revolutionary goal. By giving the learner a growing voice, their aspirations and ambitions would become central to the way services are organised. At the moment, at the heart of the system are its institutions and professions – schools and teachers – that lay down what education is and how it should proceed. Studies of performance management across a wide range of organisational fields show that productivity invariably rises when people have a role in setting and thus owning their targets. The same is true for learning.

Obstacles

The biggest challenge to the personalised services agenda is what it means for inequality. Take the case of personalised learning. Middle class homes are often far more conducive to personalised learning than many poorer homes that have less space, fewer computers and books. Thus the more that personalised learning promotes self-provisioning, the more it could widen inequalities. As more learning would be done in the pupil's own time, the state will have to work harder to equalise the conditions for learning outside school. Personalised learning will promote equity only if the resources for individualised, home-based learning are also more equally available. Personalised learning encourages us to focus on the totality of resources available for learning, at home and at school.

Middle class children do not just have more resources for learning, they and their parents probably have more time and capacity to make choices about education. Choices are made in a social context of peer and family influences. If these mitigate against learning – for example if parents had a negative experience of school, or elder siblings left school with few qualifications – then providing kids from poor, chaotic or disrupted families with *more* choice may not encourage them to consider *different* choices. Culturally and emotionally nourished children will see huge opportunities in personalised education; those who do not come from these backgrounds may not recognise the choices available to them.

The more that health and education outcomes depend on individual and private initiative, even within a public framework, the more those already well off are likely to benefit. Four in five deaths are due to circulatory disease, cancer and respiratory illnesses, in which lifestyle – diet, exercise, smoking and drinking – are the main factors. Middle class people with financial, social and emotional resources find it far easier to change their life style than poorer people who lack these resources. Public policies that depend on users making an investment of time and effort – such as smoking cessation – will favour those with relatively stable lives. It will be less favourable for those with chaotic or impoverished lives, people who struggle to get from one day to the next.

That is why the rate of smoking is declining fastest among the most well off and better educated: these are the people who are more likely to have the information, incentives and resources to change their lives. In contrast, 70 per cent of single mothers smoke. Smoking is a major cause of ill health and a drain on the public good: it costs the NHS more than £1,500 million a year to treat smoking-related disease. No public service can 'deliver' non-smoking. The decisions to start and stop smoking are made by individuals in the context of a wide range of factors, among them peer influences, advertising and emotional stress. To reduce smoking from 25 per cent of the population to, say, less than five per cent, would only be possible with a public policy that persuaded millions of people to change their lives. Public values would have to infiltrate the private domain. Yet because the capacity to make these choices is unequally distributed, so too are the outcomes. Smoking is increasingly concentrated among poorer people, while ex-smokers are more likely to be better off and better educated.

The more that services become personalised, the more public resources will have to be skewed towards the least well off to equalise opportunities. Well educated and informed consumers are already well prepared to take advantage of choice. The least well educated, informed and ambitious will need additional help to exploit the opportunities personalisation makes available to them.

These concerns should strongly influence how personalised services are designed and resourced. The role of professionals as advocates, advisers, brokers and solutions assemblers will be vital to mediate the individual's relationships with the services he or she needs. The people who most need bespoke, labour-intensive and personalised services are the most vulnerable, who are often served by multiple, poorly coordinated public services. Single mothers, children at risk, frail and elderly people should all have personal advocates to help them assemble the solutions they need from among the panoply of public service.

Moves towards user involvement and co-production are more effective when they follow a few simple rules:

○ Set incremental goals, starting small and manageably.
○ Specify clearly what the user and the service professionals expect to do.
○ Keep joint records of achievement and performance to reinforce success.
○ Give users a mix of options through which they can achieve their goals.
○ Frame the policy in an aspirational way to excite ambition.
○ Provide role models and peer-to-peer support to build confidence.

With careful design personalised services need not widen inequalities. On the contrary they could be most valuable for people in most need.

7. The politics of personalisation

A chasm has opened up between people and large organisations, both public and private.

Many people's experience of being a consumer is that they are put on hold, kept at arm's length, not told the whole story, tricked by the fine print, redirected to a website and treated like a number. We feel detached from large organisations – both public and private – that serve us in increasingly impersonal ways. While choice among commodity goods and services has expanded, the scope for personalised, human service, tailored to our needs, seems to have declined.[8]

This gap between large organisations and the intricacy of people's everyday expectations and aspirations, is a breeding ground for a growing sense of frustration and resentment, with private services as much as public. This chasm should also be the breeding ground for innovation and experimentation. That is what personalisation is about: finding innovative ways to reconnect people to the institutions that serve them.

This chasm between people and institutions is central to the future of the public sector. People may feel closely connected to and well served by their teacher, doctor or postman. But they often feel distant from the school system, the health system or the Post Office, which they see as bureaucratic and impersonal.

The debate about the future of public services is pitched into this chasm between the way public institutions work and how users experience them. Targets, league tables and inspection regimes may have improved aspects of performance in public services. Yet the cost has been to make public services seem more machine-like, more like a production line producing standardised goods.

Public service users should have a voice directly in the service as it is delivered. That voice will be unlocked only if they also have a degree of choice over when, where, how and to what end a service is delivered. The aim of personalised public services is not to provide the self-interested, self-gratification of consumerism but to build a sense of self-actualisation, self-realisation and self-enhancement. The more people are involved in making decisions about services, the more knowledgeable they become, and the more responsible and committed they become to making sure the service is a success.

Personalised services should bring wider social benefits. Users who are asked to consciously commit to goals related to a service are far more likely to stick with it, attend appointments and classes. One crime study, for example, found that people were 400 per cent more likely to intervene to stop a crime if they had pre-committed to look after the property involved. Home-school contracts work on the same principles. Involved users are likely to be more committed to a successful outcome and they are more likely to build up their own knowledge. That in turn could make them less dependent upon professionals and so less demanding. That should be good for users but also for professionals who can direct their attention elsewhere.

Across a range of activities it is increasingly clear that the state cannot deliver collective solutions from on high. It is too cumbersome and distant. The state can only help create public goods – such as better education and health – by encouraging them to emerge from within society. This is true for health, education, community safety, neighbourhood renewal and a range of other public goods.

Crime and antisocial behaviour are strongly affected by the values and behaviour of individuals, families and communities, while only modestly affected by the activities of the police and courts. In education, research suggests that variation in educational outcomes is explained by what happens at home, as much as what happens at school. More sustainable use of resources depends on changes in consumer behaviour through energy efficiency, recycling and reuse. The tax system increasingly depends on mass involvement in self-assessment and reporting.

Three million people in Britain are seriously underproviding for their pension and between five million and ten million more are not saving enough. The state cannot change their behaviour through dictat nor can it solve the problem with a better state pension. A collective solution to pensions provision will require self-regulation, new products and services and millions of people being encouraged to choose different ways to save for the future. Welfare to work and active labour market programmes are premised on the user as an active participant, who takes responsibility for building up his or her skills and contacts. Neighbourhood renewal has to come from within; it cannot be delivered top-down from the state. Most community regeneration programmes now involve local residents as participants in the process – designing and delivering change. Home care services are increasingly designed to encourage and enable elderly people to stand on their own two feet, cook, clean and look after themselves rather than provide them with a long-term service.

Participative approaches to service design and delivery create public value by recasting the relationship between the individual and the collective, the public and private. Public policy is most effective when it harnesses and shapes private activity rather than supplanting it, allowing the public good to emerge from within civil society. Personalised services are one point in a range of different ways in which public and private work together to create the public good. The state's job will be to orchestrate and enable that process, not to pretend it can provide or deliver solutions in the form of discrete services.

In more areas the onus will be on changes to private behaviour which cumulatively create public value. Anti-smoking policy is a good example. Smoking causes about a third of all cancers, about one-sixth of heart and circulatory disease and more than 80 per cent of serious lung disease. The indirect social costs of smoking – lost productivity, pain, loss and harm to non-smokers – has never been established. About 83 per cent of smokers say they would not smoke if they could have their time again. Promoting smoking cessation is a clear public good. Public policy plays a critical role in making smoking unattractive – through increased taxation, anti-smoking campaigns, restricting advertising, public information and courses which help people stop smoking. Public policy is in direct conflict with commercial interests which promote smoking at the cost of wider society. Smoking cessation cannot be delivered like a takeaway pizza. The public good – fewer people smoking – will come about through millions of individual decisions. The public good will be built bottom-up. It will come from public values and norms infiltrating private decision-making.

In other cases the public sector might provide a platform for private action.[9] There is nothing new in this. Much of nineteenth-century city government was designed to allow the public good to emerge bottom-up from within society. A prime example was the Penny Post created in 1837. The Penny Post was made possible by a dramatic expansion of the public sphere. It led to houses being numbered and streets named, through which people could be identified with their address. Yet this public and standardised system for assigning names to addresses also led to a dramatic expansion in private activity as people took up letter writing. Private communication greatly expanded on the basis of the public platform. Another example was the introduction of city maps in the nineteenth century. Before these maps were available cities were small and people navigated their way around by word of mouth and local knowledge. Maps provided an objective, standardised account of the city's shared public space. Yet maps were also simultaneously private tools for people to navigate their way around for their own purposes. Much the same could be said for water and sewerage systems and public libraries. The British state has been at its most effective when social reform has allowed public and private to expand together, with public platforms creating the basis for a complementary expansion of private endeavour.

More personalised solutions, in which the user takes responsibility for providing part of the service, should enable society to create better collective solutions with a less coercive, intrusive state, a lower tax burden, a more responsible and engaged citizenry and stronger capacity within civil society to find and devise solutions to problems without state intervention.

The logic of personalisation, if carried into the heart of public organisation, will have far-reaching consequences.

The chief challenge facing government in a liberal, open society is how to help create public goods – such as a well educated population, with an appetite to learn – in a society with a democratic ethos, which prizes individual freedom and wants to be self-organising and 'bottom-up'. Government cannot decide on its definition of the public good and impose it from above, at least not continually. It cannot simply regulate smoking, poor reading and bad eating habits out of existence. Nor can it stand back and accept whatever emerges from complex, self-organising systems, such as education and health, in which there are many relatively autonomous players. The British secondary education system, if left to its own self-organising devices, would likely entrench underachievement and low aspirations, as well as provide some with greater opportunities for learning.

The English state in particular is caught in a bind: committed to protecting, even expanding, the sphere of private freedom it also is necessarily committed to shaping, continuously, how people use their freedom in the name of the public good. In an open, self-organising society, government has to become molecular: it has to get into the bloodstream of society, not impose change or deliver solutions from without. Government is exercised in a myriad of micro settings, and often not just by state employees but by teachers, experts, advisers, parents, volunteers and peers. Most of the work of government is not conducted in departments in Whitehall but at thousands of points scattered across society.

The challenge then is not just to personalise

services but to shift from a model in which the centre controls, initiates, plans, instructs and serves, to one in which the centre governs through promoting collaborative, critical and honest self-evaluation and self-improvement. Reforms to public services should drive in this direction promoting new sources of information for users, creating new interfaces such as NHS Direct for them to access services and get advice, providing professionals with the skills and support to become brokers and advisers as well as solutions providers, changing funding regimes to give users more influence over how money is spent on the services they consume, giving users a right to a voice in the design of the services they use.

A state that is committed to protecting private freedom must also continuously shape how people use their freedom in the name of the wider public good. Personalisation through participation is part of the solution to this dilemma of how to rule through freedom, to allow the public good to be created within society rather than relying on the state to deliver it.

Notes

1. Anne Rhodes' story and seven other case studies of public services innovation are told in C Leadbeater, *The Man in the Caravan and other stories* (Hayes, Mddx: IDeA Publications, 2003).

2. For further reading on scripts, services and innovation see B Nooteboom, *Learning and Innovation in Organisations and Economies* (Oxford: Oxford University Press, 2001).

3. See G Kelly and S Muers, *Creating Public Value: an analytical framework for public service reform* (London: Strategy Unit, Cabinet Office, 2002), available at: www.strategy.gov.uk.

4. Speech on 12 Dec 2003 to launch of *The Adaptive State: strategies for personalising the public realm* (London, Demos, 2003).

5. See *Creating Public Value*, Strategy Unit.

6. D Halpern and C Bates with G Beales and A Heathfield, *Personal Responsibility and Changing Behaviour: the state of knowledge and its implications for public policy*, discussion paper (London: Strategy Unit, Cabinet Office, 2004).

7.   T Bentley, *The Self Creating Society* (Renewal, 2004),
      available at www.renewal.org.uk.
8.   J Maxmin and S Zuboff, *The Support Economy: why
      corporations are failing individuals and the next episode
      of capitalism* (London: Allen Lane/Penguin, 2003).
9.   See P Joyce, *The Rule of Freedom: liberalism and the
      modern city* (New York: Verso, 2003); and N Rose,
      Powers of Freedom: reframing political thought
      (Cambridge: Cambridge University Press, 1999).

DEMOS – Licence to Publish

2. **Fair Use Rights.** Nothing in this licence is intended to reduce, limit, or restrict any rights arising from fair use, first sale or other limitations on the exclusive rights of the copyright owner under copyright law or other applicable laws.

3. **Licence Grant.** Subject to the terms and conditions of this Licence, Licensor hereby grants You a worldwide, royalty-free, non-exclusive, perpetual (for the duration of the applicable copyright) licence to exercise the rights in the Work as stated below:

   a to reproduce the Work, to incorporate the Work into one or more Collective Works, and to reproduce the Work as incorporated in the Collective Works;

   b to distribute copies or phonorecords of, display publicly, perform publicly, and perform publicly by means of a digital audio transmission the Work including as incorporated in Collective Works;

   The above rights may be exercised in all media and formats whether now known or hereafter devised. The above rights include the right to make such modifications as are technically necessary to exercise the rights in other media and formats. All rights not expressly granted by Licensor are hereby reserved.

4. **Restrictions.** The licence granted in Section 3 above is expressly made subject to and limited by the following restrictions:

   a You may distribute, publicly display, publicly perform, or publicly digitally perform the Work only under the terms of this Licence, and You must include a copy of, or the Uniform Resource Identifier for, this Licence with every copy or phonorecord of the Work You distribute, publicly display, publicly perform, or publicly digitally perform. You may not offer or impose any terms on the Work that alter or restrict the terms of this Licence or the recipients' exercise of the rights granted hereunder. You may not sublicence the Work. You must keep intact all notices that refer to this Licence and to the disclaimer of warranties. You may not distribute, publicly display, publicly perform, or publicly digitally perform the Work with any technological measures that control access or use of the Work in a manner inconsistent with the terms of this Licence Agreement. The above applies to the Work as incorporated in a Collective Work, but this does not require the Collective Work apart from the Work itself to be made subject to the terms of this Licence. If You create a Collective Work, upon notice from any Licencor You must, to the extent practicable, remove from the Collective Work any reference to such Licensor or the Original Author, as requested.

b You may not exercise any of the rights granted to You in Section 3 above in any manner that is primarily intended for or directed toward commercial advantage or private monetary compensation. The exchange of the Work for other copyrighted works by means of digital file-sharing or otherwise shall not be considered to be intended for or directed toward commercial advantage or private monetary compensation, provided there is no payment of any monetary compensation in connection with the exchange of copyrighted works.

c If you distribute, publicly display, publicly perform, or publicly digitally perform the Work or any Collective Works, You must keep intact all copyright notices for the Work and give the Original Author credit reasonable to the medium or means You are utilizing by conveying the name (or pseudonym if applicable) of the Original Author if supplied; the title of the Work if supplied. Such credit may be implemented in any reasonable manner; provided, however, that in the case of a Collective Work, at a minimum such credit will appear where any other comparable authorship credit appears and in a manner at least as prominent as such other comparable authorship credit.

5. Representations, Warranties and Disclaimer

a By offering the Work for public release under this Licence, Licensor represents and warrants that, to the best of Licensor's knowledge after reasonable inquiry:

i Licensor has secured all rights in the Work necessary to grant the licence rights hereunder and to permit the lawful exercise of the rights granted hereunder without You having any obligation to pay any royalties, compulsory licence fees, residuals or any other payments;

ii The Work does not infringe the copyright, trademark, publicity rights, common law rights or any other right of any third party or constitute defamation, invasion of privacy or other tortious injury to any third party.

b EXCEPT AS EXPRESSLY STATED IN THIS LICENCE OR OTHERWISE AGREED IN WRITING OR REQUIRED BY APPLICABLE LAW, THE WORK IS LICENCED ON AN "AS IS" BASIS, WITHOUT WARRANTIES OF ANY KIND, EITHER EXPRESS OR IMPLIED INCLUDING, WITHOUT LIMITATION, ANY WARRANTIES REGARDING THE CONTENTS OR ACCURACY OF THE WORK.

6. **Limitation on Liability.** EXCEPT TO THE EXTENT REQUIRED BY APPLICABLE LAW, AND EXCEPT FOR DAMAGES ARISING FROM LIABILITY TO A THIRD PARTY RESULTING FROM BREACH OF THE WARRANTIES IN SECTION 5, IN NO EVENT WILL LICENSOR BE LIABLE TO YOU ON ANY LEGAL THEORY FOR ANY SPECIAL, INCIDENTAL, CONSEQUENTIAL, PUNITIVE OR EXEMPLARY DAMAGES ARISING OUT OF THIS LICENCE OR THE USE OF THE WORK, EVEN IF LICENSOR HAS BEEN ADVISED OF THE POSSIBILITY OF SUCH DAMAGES.

7. **Termination**

   a   This Licence and the rights granted hereunder will terminate automatically upon any breach by You of the terms of this Licence. Individuals or entities who have received Collective Works from You under this Licence, however, will not have their licences terminated provided such individuals or entities remain in full compliance with those licences. Sections 1, 2, 5, 6, 7, and 8 will survive any termination of this Licence.

   b   Subject to the above terms and conditions, the licence granted here is perpetual (for the duration of the applicable copyright in the Work). Notwithstanding the above, Licensor reserves the right to release the Work under different licence terms or to stop distributing the Work at any time; provided, however that any such election will not serve to withdraw this Licence (or any other licence that has been, or is required to be, granted under the terms of this Licence), and this Licence will continue in full force and effect unless terminated as stated above.

8.   Miscellaneous

   a   Each time You distribute or publicly digitally perform the Work or a Collective Work, DEMOS offers to the recipient a licence to the Work on the same terms and conditions as the licence granted to You under this Licence.

   b   If any provision of this Licence is invalid or unenforceable under applicable law, it shall not affect the validity or enforceability of the remainder of the terms of this Licence, and without further action by the parties to this agreement, such provision shall be reformed to the minimum extent necessary to make such provision valid and enforceable.

   c   No term or provision of this Licence shall be deemed waived and no breach consented to unless such waiver or consent shall be in writing and signed by the party to be charged with such waiver or consent.

d This Licence constitutes the entire agreement between the parties with respect to the Work licensed here. There are no understandings, agreements or representations with respect to the Work not specified here. Licensor shall not be bound by any additional provisions that may appear in any communication from You. This Licence may not be modified without the mutual written agreement of DEMOS and You.